D0504171

The Herald

IT'S A SIGN!

UNBELIEVABLE SIGNS FROM SCOTLAND AND BEYOND

Edited by Ken Smith

BLACK & WHITE PUBLISHING

First published 2012
by Black & White Publishing Ltd
29 Ocean Drive, Edinburgh EH6 6JL

3 5 7 9 10 8 6 4 2   13 14 15

ISBN: 978 1 84502 419 2

A CIP catalogue record for this book
is available from the British Library.

Designed by Richard Budd Design
Printed and bound in Poland
www.hussarbooks.pl

CONTENTS

INTRODUCTION

It's a strange phenomenon that, as the ability to take instant photographs with small digital cameras and many mobile phones has increased, the number of photographs of the Loch Ness Monster and alien spacecraft has decreased. Perhaps the loch's creature and the visitors from other planets have suddenly become camera-shy.

However, one area that has benefited from this rise in instant photography is the Diary column in *The Herald* newspaper. In the past readers would describe an amusing sign or view and end the description with the phrase, 'If only I had a camera with me.' Now almost all of us have become instant photographers by simply reaching into a pocket for a mobile phone, pointing it, and taking a snap. Nor do we need to know what an f-stop is in a camera's aperture scale. Point the phone or digital camera, press a button and that's it.

The only time you hear f-stop nowadays is when a Glasgow drunk is making enquiries about where he can catch a bus.

So for years now *The Herald*'s Diary column has been recording the daft signs, mis-spellings, and visual oddities sent in by our generous readers who have indeed reached for that phone or camera.

Thank you to all our readers for their help. Here are a few of the more popular ones.

CHAPTER 1

SCOTTISH DIALECTS

Scots may speak the Queen's English - sometimes - but that doesn't stop them from wandering off into their own dialects, slang, and pronunciations. Thus it may seem perfectly acceptable in South Africa to have a bank called Nedbank, but to visiting Scots it conjures up pictures of skinny wee pasty-faced individuals in Burberry caps drinking bottles of Buckie while depositing their giro cheques.

Here are some other examples of pictures that only make Scots laugh.

MING INN
Lunch Pack Special

12 TO 2.30PM

$**6.30**

GST INCLUDED

TAKEAWAY ONLY

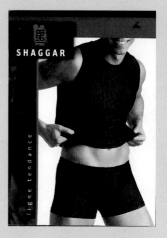

SHAGGAR

ligne tendance

THE OLDEST CHURCH IN PARIS - XIIth century
1, rue St-Julien-le-Pauvre - Paris 5e (150 m de Notre-Dame) Mo St-Michel - N.D. ou Maubert

JEUDI 21 AOÛT à 20H30
THURSDAY AUGUST 21 8.30PM

CHOPIN LISZT

Rhapsodies Hongroises n° 2, 6...
Rêve d'Amour (Liebestraum),
La Campanella, Nocturnes, Valses, Etudes ...

par Herbert du Plessis, piano (**Steinway**)

Prix des Places : Normales : 18€ - Étudiants : 13€ - 1ère Cat. : 23€
Locations : FNAC - VIRGIN - G. LAFAYETTE - BON MARCHÉ
Tél 01 42 26 00 00 - Billets à l'église, une heure avant le concert

FOR SALE
SE VENDE

GLASGOW

JIMMY'IZ GYROS

Coca-Cola

FROG PORRIDGE

TOILETS

→ → → → →

LOCH LOMOND & THE TROSSACHS NATIONAL PARK

HAVE YOU DROPPED ONE?

KEEP THE NATIONAL PARK LITTER FREE

TAKE IT HOME

Community Partnership

design
centre

KITCHEN FLAIR

poggen
pohl

PRESS BELL

Fearann an Leagha
Fernilea

Port nan Long
Portnalong

Fiosgabhaig
Fiskavaig

CHURCH OF SCOTLAND

MINGINISH
TOURIST
ROUTE

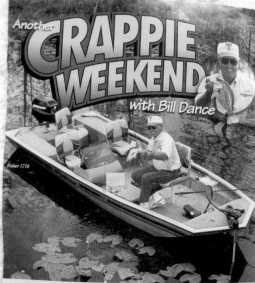

Another CRAPPIE WEEKEND
with Bill Dance

Fisher 1710

Fisher 1600

Fish Forever

$7,495

Let the fun begin! Specifically designed for crappie fishermen, these babies show no mercy. You'll go crappie happy with all the 1710 has to offer. From the tough all welded hull to all the fishing extras — like aerated livewells, baitwells, Lowrance® X-58 depth finder and an

XP-4000 trolling motor by MotorGuide® you've got just one heckuva crappie boat. **For all the "specs" visit** www.fisherboats.com. **Or call toll-free,** 1-888-669-2248.

Fisher Boats
Boats Of A Lifetime

HOTEL DE LA HERSE D'OR

20

HOTEL HERSE D'OR

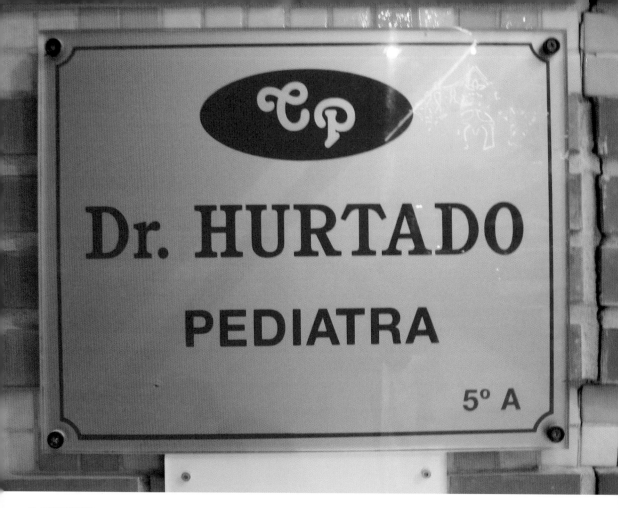

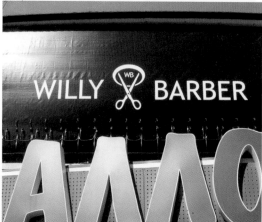

El - Nashar
Dental Care Ltd
www.el-nashar.co.uk
Tel: 01626 212121

If staff suspect you are Supplying alcohol or cigarettes to minors you will only be served once a day.

IMPORTANT NOTICE

Great Barrier Island

Coromandel Walkway

CHAPTER 2

SCOTLAND

Diary readers don't always have to travel far for an amusing sign. Only a council worker would think nothing of erecting a tourist sign for a safari park that wants to attract visitors, directly below a large sign for the village of Dull.

In other places, while graffiti artists are to be condemned, they have nevertheless added to our amusement by the judicious adding of a word or two to a sign. It was surely inevitable that the road sign for the village, Crook of Devon would have added below it, 'Twinned with the Thief of Baghdad'.

Here are some more examples.

MAY 2006 PROMOTION

Delice de France

Healthy Option!!

*Purchase any Can of
Juice and a
Traditional Scotch
Pie for *only*
£1.00*

ALMONDCATERING

WANTY STOP
PISHIN IN THE
CLOSE YA MANKY
SHOWER OF
BASTARDS...!

WARNING

STAFF MAY APPEAR GRUMPIER DUE TO LACK OF PASSIVE-SMOKING

~

THANK YOU FOR YOUR PATIENCE THROUGH THIS TIME OF TRANSITION xXx

Sale

Large Discounts on All

Men's Bottoms

alpine bikes

Litter/Vandalism/Rubbish
☐ A big problem   ☐   A problem

People using or dealing drugs
☐ A big problem   ☐   A problem

People being drunk or rowdy
☐ A big problem   ☐   A problem

4 How satisfied are you with my work as your local MP?

(1= very satisfied, 5= very satisfied)   1☐   2☐   3☐

5 Would you like a copy of my "keep warm this winter -
sent to you? Please tick ☐ yes ☐ no

our details

Full name: Addre

Tel:

Sale on view

opening hours

Monday	10.00am- 12.30pm 1.30pm - 4.00pm
Tuesday	closed
Wednesday	closed
Thursday	10.00am- 12.30pm 1.30pm - 4.00pm
Friday	10.00am- 12.30pm 1.30pm - 4.00pm

always open!

Bank of Scotland: 08457 801801
bankofscotland.co.uk

Halifax: 08457 394959
halifax.co.uk

£2,50

Bank of Scotland: Lost/stolen cards telephone: 0131 549 8046

Civilian Marmalade Oranges

DANGER
KEEP
OUT

WELCOME
TO THE
SOUTHERN NECROPOLIS

All business transferred to

The Tanning Shop

14 Fade Street

beside the market bar
phone: 679 8929

NO DOGS
ALLOWED
(except guide dogs)

RULE 2

ALL CHILDREN
MUST WEAR
SAFETY BELTS
AROUND THEIR
WASTE

RULE 3

DRIVE ONE WAY
AROUND THE TRACK

SHEEP
PLEASE KEEP
DOGS ON LEASH

O-WHEELED TRAFFIC

Bananas

From ~~Fife~~ Fyfes

£1.75/kg

baby needs
beers & wines

The co-operative

PEOPLE FROM EDINBURGH WELCOME (ISH)

Glosgow: Scotlan with sty

LIVE IN STAFF

NO SMOKING
NO CREDIT CARDS
NO MOBILE PHONES
NO CAMERAS
NO BACKPACKERS

bam
Viewing
gallery

WOULD ALL GOLFERS
PLEASE ENSURE THAT
ITEMS OF CLOTHING ETC.
ARE REMOVED BEFORE
CLOSING TIME

THANK YOU

CRAMS BAR

BEST

NAE
NUMPTIES
ALLOWED

Ice Rink Closed
Due to
Inclement Weather

aye it wis

WI SNY

CLEARANCE SALE

Mother of the Bride
from £50

LADIES

Uig Harbour

Raasay Pier Old Toilets

These toilets are now closed. Nearest public toilets are at the new ferry terminal. Sorry for any inconvenience-now cross your legs.

Details of key holder phone 01470 542381

GLASGOW NEWS

September 2011 Issue 30

SP Publications

Tel: 0141 954 6030

236 Ayr Road, Newton
Tel: 0141 616 2624

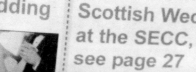

SOUTH GLASGOW YOUTH ARRESTED FOR 'INTICING RIOTS'

16-year-old boy appeared in a Glasgow sheriff court for allegedly inciting riots using Facebook.

STRATHCLYDE police said the youth was detained following a raid on a property in the south of the city on Tuesday after a posting appeared on a Facebook inviting people to follow the rioting and looting in English cities.

It emerged on Tuesday a Facebook user, Cessnock

The page was closed down after other Facebook users in Glasgow attacked his actions, adding phone numbers for Crimestoppers and reporting him to Facebook.

Strathclyde police said it had no intelligence to suggest there was any trouble planned

CHAPTER 3

MORE FROM ABROAD

Travelling on a plane, as someone once said, is nature's way of making you look like your passport photograph. Fortunately most Scots, in order to avoid an entire year of rain, cloud and cold winds, will put up with airports in order to venture abroad once a year for their fortnight in the sun. While there they are attuned to the differences and subtle nuances in a foreign language. In other words, if it makes them laugh, they'll take a picture.

At the Diary we sometimes wonder whether something as innocuous as say The Airdrie Savings Bank is actually Serbo-Croat for 'Your Sister Is A Tubby' and every week smiling Croatians take pictures outside it.

Anyway here are some of our favourite holiday snaps from abroad.

VOX

DURING HAPPY HOUR FROM 5,30 pm TO 9 pm
BOTTLES OF WINE WILL COST € 4.00 EXTRA

RED WINE

- Piemonte
  - DOLCETTO D'ALBA TRE VIGNE   VIETTI   € 18,00
  - BARBERA D'ALBA TRE VIGNE   VIETTI   € 20,00

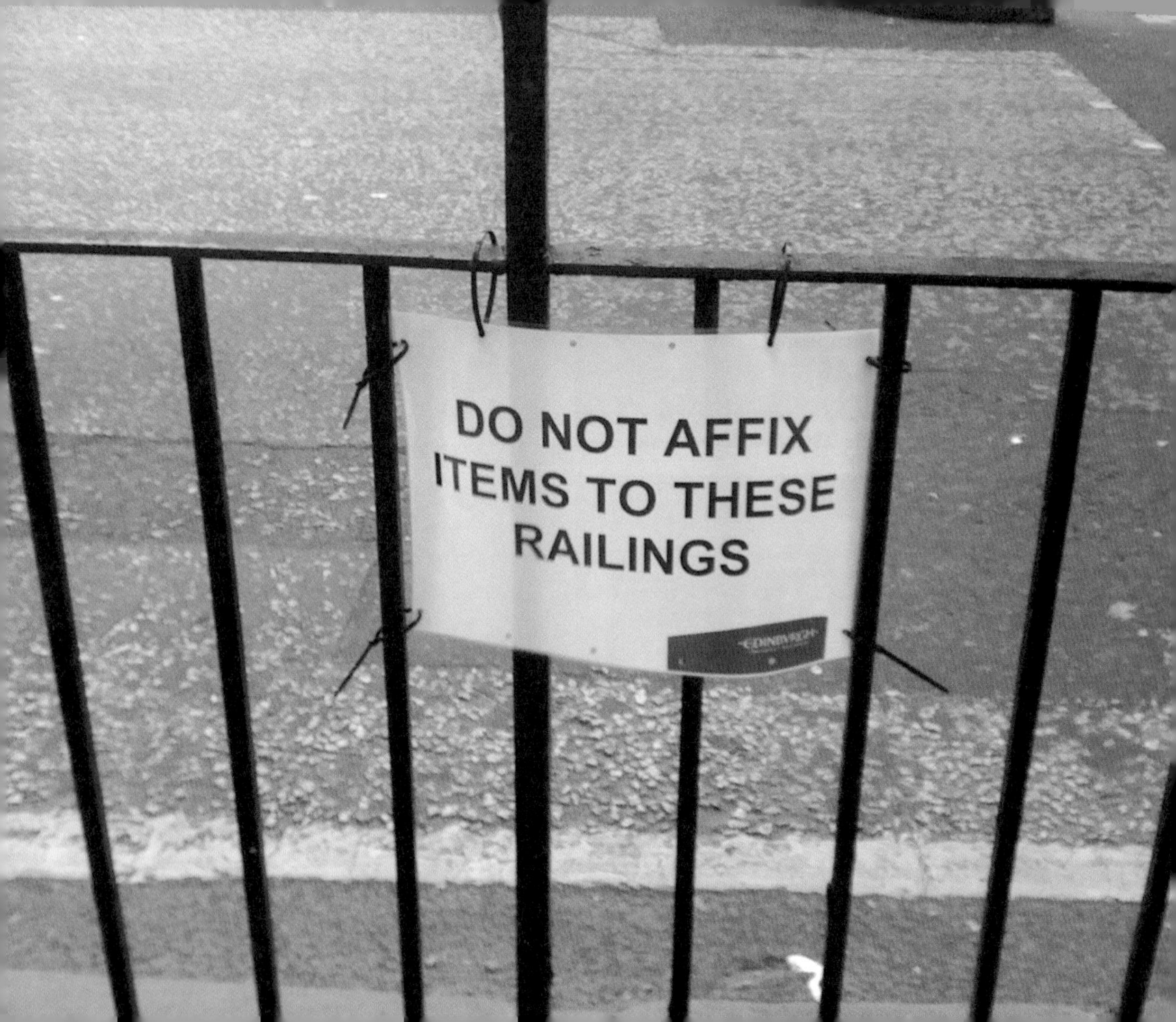
DO NOT AFFIX
ITEMS TO THESE
RAILINGS

CHAPTER 4
OTHER SIGNS

Nor do we forget our cousins south of the border, where many of these signs and notices were snapped.

TONNA
COMMUNITY COUNCIL
DOG
SKATEBOARDING
ALLOWED

EVERY TIME A CYCLIST
JUMPS A RED LIGHT
GOD KILLS A KITTEN

BABY & TODDLER
HANGING ROOM

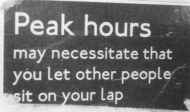

Peak hours
may necessitate that
you let other people
sit on your lap

SIN
PLACE

KEEP THE GRAVEYARD
TIDY USE THE
BINS PROVIDED

JESUS SAID
HE THAT DRINKETH OF THIS
WATER SHALL THIRST AGAIN
BUT WHOSOEVER DRINKETH
OF THE WATER THAT I SHALL
GIVE HIM SHALL NEVER
THIRST

This water is not suitable for human consumption.

JENNINGS THE OAKS HOTEL JENNINGS

JENNINGS
CAR
PARK
AT RE...
← ...
FAMILIES WELCOME

OAP ROAST SPECIAL
ONLY £3.50
MON-FRI 12-2

St. Cyril of Alexandria
CATHOLIC CHURCH
STAYING IN BED
SHOUTING, OH GOD !
DOES NOT CONSTITUTE
GOING TO CHURCH
DIOCESE OF GALVESTON-HOUSTON

CHAPTER 5

MAKE US LAUGH THEN

Many of the signs sent by our readers were not of course meant to be funny, and only became so because of dropped letters, unusual translations, or the coincidence of them looking Scottish. We give an honourable mention though to business owners or members of the public who deliberately go for humour to catch the eye.

PLEASE NOTE

DUE TO CIRCUMSTANCES BEYOND
OUR CONTROL

NORMAL WORKING WILL CONTINUE
UNTIL FURTHER NOTICE

OPEN

CLAUDE
PRESBYTERIAN CHURCH

THERE ARE SOME
QUESTIONS THAT
CAN'T BE
ANSWERED BY
GOOGLE

GOODWOOD UNITED CHURCH

FREE COFFEE
EVERLASTING LIFE
YES MEMBERSHIP HAS
ITS PRIVILEGES

SERVICE 9:30   640-1781   REV. ELAINE LUSH, M.DIV.

Voted
Lib-Dem?
Never Mind!

Staropramen
£20
a
Case!

YOUR HUSBAND CALLED
AND SAID YOU CAN BUY ANYTHING YOU WANT

PICKWICKS TAVERN

HUSBAND CREĆHE

DOES HE ANNOY YOU ON THE BEACH?

GET UNDER YOUR FEET AS YOU SHOP?

WHY NOT LEAVE HIM HERE

AND PICK HIM UP LATER?

NO CHARGE, JUST BUY HIS DRINKS

CAUTION
ALLIGATOR
MATING SEASON

If Attacked,
fake orgasm

TODAY'S TRESPASSER
IS
TOMORROW'S
ROTTWEILER SHIT

CHAPTER 6
FINALLY

A final chapter of those that are hard to categorise, but nevertheless make us smile.

BEWARE OF THE

I've got nothing against God
It's his Fan Club I can't stand

POT HOLING

Bungee Jumpers
Assembly Point

The Quest for the Phoenix's Nest

Follow the Clues and Discover the Nest of The Legendary Phoenix

Get your Quest Sheet from the Office

Herbalist Demonstration

Find out how plants found in our woods can b
used for health and nutrition

12:00 to 4:00 in the Square

Cancelled due to illness

Tra

FOR SALE

PARACHUTE

USED ONCE - UNOPENED

£299 O.N.O

07931 46158

the bit waiting for that breakthrough to happen this year.

Career, relationship, home or way of life – whether you choose to make the changes yourself or whether change is thrust upon you, the first thing you can

...personal... your rush to adventure and your need to overthrow the old for the new will sometimes bring out your impatient side.

Don't end up throwing the baby out with the bath water.

thrill of the unk...

Even if you ar physically you v broaden your in In this time you more, develop y

TAURUS APRIL 21 - MAY 21

There will be much activity taking place behind the scenes for you this year and over the next seven years as you develop new ideas. What you are doing is preparing foundations and building yourself a solid core for the future.

Although it's not like you to daydream you will now find yourself drifting off into reveries. Don't stop this, allow your mind to go into free fall because that is what will give your subconscious time to work

and to come up with those amazing flashes of inspiration.

If you wonder where all those bright ideas, inventions and intuitive insights are coming from, it's Uranus.

Your dreams are also likely to be more colourful and in some cases prophetic. Listen to your intuition and follow through but beware of nervous strain and take extra care of your legs. Poor footwear could lead to pulled muscles and sprains.

VIRGO A

Emotionally the No the easiest for you difficult and your lo turbulent but with ti Uranus from your p you should find that now settle down an for emotional happi encouraging.

Where your attent and through to 2018 finances and busine could be sudden gai

GEMINI MAY 22 - JUNE 21

From now through to 2018 it's all about who you know. You will find yourself forming new friendships and associations over the next seven years and gravitating towards a whole new crowd.

...most people you will meet

world and bring unexpected advantages and benefits.

If you are single it could be that you find a soul-mate among them or else an existing friendship grows into something deeper. You will also start to re-think your long-term goals and

LIBRA SEP

Close personal rela under the spotlig expect changes your relationshi volatile, exciting change your sta Happily

Boyzone to play gig in Inverness

BOYZONE is the latest big name band to announce a Highland date.

The original Irish boy band, which has sold over 15 records worldwide, will appear at the Northern Meeting Park in Inverness on Saturday 27th August.

Former "X Factor" winner Shane Ward will provide the support for Boyzone in front of 12,000 people at the city centre venue.

Salmon sworn in as First Minister

SNP leader Alex Salmond was yesterday sworn in as Scotland's new First Minister. Mr Salmond took the oaths of office at the Court of Session in Edinburgh. He was watched by 15 of the country's most senior judges, before signing the formal documents sealing his appointment. The Nationalist leader later headed to Holyrood where he sought the approval of MSPs for his list of ministerial nominees.

Crowds invaded Downing Street yesterday, hoping that Mr. Churchill would make an appearance.

100,000 British Troops in Germany Go Gay

TOASTS TO THE FALLEN, AND TO LASTING PEACE

VE-Day was celebrated by over 100,000 British troops in Germany with bonfires, Verey lights of a dozen colours, and festivities in every mess and billet from the Weser to the Rhine, from the Rhine to the Elbe, and from the Baltic to Brussels.

Lights blazed from unshut- | from a balcony outside the British

SINKO INTERNATIONAL

YACHT SUPPLIER

FRENCH RIVIERA

MONACO · VILLEFRANCHE · MENTON · CANNES · NICE
EZE · ST JEAN CAP FERRAT · ANTIBES · ST TROPEZ
SINKO-INTERNATIONAL.COM
+33 (0) 618.63.68.40

Summer

Lake Garda

07 nights **Half bored**

From **£290**

Per **person** based on **02** sharing.

Includes: resort transfers

Staying at: **riviera** Departing: **gatwick** on: **17/07/2010**

Key Information: